A SPLIT SECOND OF LIGHT

A BOOK OF POETRY
BY
STEWART FLORSHEIM

BLUE LIGHT PRESS ◆ 1ST WORLD PUBLISHING

1st WORLD
PUBLISHING

SAN FRANCISCO ◆ FAIRFIELD ◆ DELHI

1ST WORLD LIBRARY
809 S. 2nd Street
Fairfield, IA 52556
www.1stworldpublishing.com

BLUE LIGHT PRESS
1563 45th Avenue
San Francisco, California, 94122

BOOK & COVER DESIGN
Melanie Gendron
www.melaniegendron.com

COVER, AUTHOR & INTERIOR PHOTOGRAPHY
Leon Borensztein

FIRST EDITION

LCCN: 2011924997

ISBN: 978-1-4218-8605-3

A SPLIT SECOND OF LIGHT

ACKNOWLEDGEMENTS

"Game Board" appeared in *Compassion and Choices Magazine,* Summer 2007

"Testifying Before the Judiciary Committee" appeared in *Compassion and Choices Magazine,* Summer 2008

"Mother's Favorite Drawing" appeared in *The Pedestal Magazine,* Issue 45, April, 2008

"Green Balloons" and "Encounter" appeared in *Psychological Perspectives: A Semiannual Journal of Jungian Thought,* Volume 51, Issue 2, 2008

"The Turning" appeared in *Glass: A Journal of Poetry,* Volume 2, Issue 3, December, 2009

"The Machine" appeared in *The Pedestal Magazine,* Issue 55, December, 2009

"Summer Camp," "The Boy Scout Handbook," and "Mother Wants to Know" appeared in *FutureCycle,* December, 2009, and in *FutureCycle Poetry: Poems for the Ages,* Future Cycle Press, 2010

"Statement Recording the Property of Jews" and "Last Words" appeared in *From the Well of Living Waters,* Kehilla Community Synagogue, 2011

Sincere thanks to Jannie Dresser, Diane Frank, and Scott Norton for reviewing the final draft of this book, and to the writers who critiqued many of these poems in workshops. My gratitude to Maureen and Robert Barker for awarding me a residency at Artcroft, where many of the poems in this collection were completed. And my deep appreciation to my wife, Judy Rosloff, and my daughters, Orli and Maya, for their support and inspiration.

In Memory of Joe Rosloff

The red cardinal
tries to fly in
through a window,
its small heart
beating wildly:
the soul of a man
who knows
he will not
return home.

TABLE OF CONTENTS

2

3

God can be whatever you want,
a broken mirror
that sees all aspects at once

—from "The Canal," by Frances Richey (from *The Warrior*)

BEGINNING

Mother and Father scream at each other: the riveting silence.
Every night when I am a boy, I whisper the *Sh'ma.*

A few days before I become a Bar Mitzvah, Mother loses her voice.
In the *Psalms,* the splendors of the universe.

In Kathmandu I walk around a stupa, twirl prayer bells.
A solid bronze door opens: a dazzling glow.

A pinhole of light appears through the clouds.
We come across a field: whirlpools, oak trees, cyclamen.

Mornings I take my dog for a walk in the cemetery.
The *Zohar* says nothing is known beyond the infinite so it is
    called Beginning.

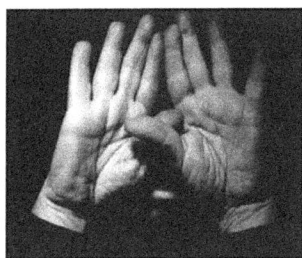

1

It is not in the heavens.

—Deuteronomy 30:12

MOTHER'S FAVORITE DRAWING

I am with her when she sees the drawing
at the gift shop after I drag her through the Met—

a 12-year-old teaching his mother about the great things
in New York besides Ellis Island.

It's the Käthe Kollwitz of a woman clutching
her child—my mother interrogating the child's eyes

for something familiar: the shadow of an old man just before
the dreamer awakens, the pattern of a favorite school dress,

the arc of a uniformed arm before it smacks her in the head,
the color of the suitcase her father lifts off the floor.

Mother never buys on impulse but doesn't hesitate—
she even gets it matted and framed in brass

and we carry it home on the #4 bus, Mother gripping the bar
with one hand, the picture secured between her legs.

Back in our building, the elevator broken as usual,
we carry the picture up four floors

past other apartments also filled with survivors,
walls bare as ours, and before we take off our coats

Mother wants to hang it over her bed in a spot
framed now by the shadow of the fire escape,

the steps and ladder imposed over mother and child
bracing them forever in flight.

THE SACRED

1.

I forgive my father, his propensity
to believe in things he can't know.
This afternoon I was riveted to a painting—
a nude staring into morning light,
the long shadow she decided to leave
behind, the bed next to her unmade,
red high-heeled shoes resting at right angles.
Art, we say, because it redeems us
not unlike the woman in the painting
who had more lovers than she can recall—
each one always the last.

2.

Father in temple praying loudly
in language he does not understand.
When he starts bowing with the other men
I'm the one who gets dizzy so I place him
back in his meat market, imagine
he's picking up sides of beef
to hand to God. We walk home,
my hand tucked inside his and nothing
can faze us—even Mother who starts
yelling at Father as we enter the apartment
wondering how he can expect to be saved.

SCENES

Writing in my room alone
Mother barges in—
You think too much—
as though my thoughts might
betray her or I might miss
some of the words she hurls at Father,
You're so stupid, why don't you go back
to Hünfeld with the chickens and cows.
My room is tiny and only has
a plastic accordion door
but I unfold it with ceremony,
a Japanese screen with waterfalls,
cloud-covered mountains
and people who speak softly
in voices I can understand.

THE BOY SCOUT HANDBOOK

Father makes a big loop
then pulls the end of the rope through.
It looks like a cursive *O,*
the first letter of a word
in a foreign language
we're trying to master
but neither of us has a clue:
bowline, clove hitch, sheet bend.
He looks at the book
then pulls the rope out,
sweating—his big hands
that would sooner carve sides of beef.
Years earlier he took me
to his meat market
and showed off the carcasses
hanging in the locker.
See, this is how you carve a steak,
from the hindquarter.
His cleaver glided easily
across lines of gristle
then he handed me the filet,
blood dripping
from his hands into mine.

ACCOMMODATING THE LIGHT

after the painting, *Boy in a Striped Sweater,*
by Amedeo Modigliani, 1918

The boy wants to go out to play but his mother insists:
she marches to the closet and takes out the pin-striped sweater
she selected the week before, the pressed pants.
He groans as she buttons his sweater,
zips his fly and walks him into the salon
where he'll have to sit for hours,
adjusting only to accommodate the light.
The boy smells the grass, feels the sun, his cleats
gripping the earth then he kicks back his leg,
hears his friends cheer—this time
the ball makes it past the goalie.
His mother stands behind the painter and smiles but
she worries her son won't be able to hold his own
with the bigger boys and his math grades won't improve.
He's far too sensitive and she can see that clearly
as the light reaches his eyes and they become so transparent
she wants to run over to hold him and never let go.

Hired Help

Mother just out of the hospital after a hysterectomy
and still my sister and I can't believe our luck.
The apartment is so small we bump into Mrs. Nelson
as we follow her around, unable to imagine how she'll
improve our tidy home. She irons towels, underwear
and the bathroom becomes so sanitized we pretend
Mr. Clean has moved in and wiped away the usual smells
from our floor—*gribenes* and *schmaltz*.
We invite our friends over for foods we never knew—
southern-fried chicken, plantains, black-eyed peas—
most of them wondering how bananas could taste so
good but we save the biggest thrill for last.
We cross the street to the bus station, dig out a dime
and huddle around the pay phone receiver
as the ringing stops, Mrs. Nelson picks up
and clears her voice: *The Florsheim Residence.*

RELIGIOUS SCHOOL LESSONS

We're twelve-years old, reading the part of *Genesis*
where Lot has drunken sex with his daughters
when Carol passes a note across the room to Roger:
What do you think about fucking?
The note is only folded once so we're sure
we're supposed to read it, the words burning
a path across wide-open eyes. We don't see
Mr. Bohrer making his way to the end
of the receiving line and instead of using this
as a lesson about the great themes in the *Torah*,
he pulls up Carol and Roger by the ears
holding them as though they have the plague.
When they leave for the rabbi's the banter begins:
Lot didn't know he was screwing his daughters.
Is that what wine does to you? Gross!
Whatever, his kids must've been cretins.
Steven makes the note into a paper airplane
that lands on the ceiling light and we imagine
it will descend during the Sabbath service—
a question from the heavens.

SCHMULTZE'S

In camp the new boy approaches me
and asks if he can be my friend.
I know he's the one they'll pick on
the way some classmates found our teacher's
white cashmere cardigan and one by one
pulled off each mother-of-pearl button.
She was the nicest teacher we had.
I tell the boy I'm not sure yet
but something in his eyes draws me in:
the reflection of the field ahead,
the road that leads to Schmultze's,
the abandoned house we explore each summer—
front door on one hinge, torn screen,
the bedroom with a single box spring
and slashed mattress on the floor,
the kitchen with a sink full of dirty dishes,
open mustard jar alongside its crusted lid:
the small wooden table set for one person.

SUMMER CAMP

We line up to play bombardment
and everyone wants to be on
Bobby Thewman's team.
We know the rage in his eyes
as he pulls back his right arm,
the white ball suddenly not a white ball.
We've all had it hurled into our stomachs,
the greasy breakfast eggs an unwanted return.
We go back to the same camp in the Catskills
every year, children of survivors
from the same German-Jewish 'hood—
so we can name the perpetrators,
hear them screaming in a language
we speak to our families, identify
our grandparents in photos and letters.

We're stunned when Bobby Thewman
doesn't return one June.
He moved in with relatives across the country,
his parents having made a pact:
his father firing the first of two shots.

TRANSMIGRATIONS

Jewish mystics believe Cain came back as Jethro.
In my dreams, my sister turns and saves me from drowning.

Hamlet begins to see through the heavens.
Dubious legacy: a universe without boundaries.

My first born is named after my grandmother.
Breath reassembles into a word.

A man on the train says he wants to come back as his dog.
In the park, a man and his bulldog frown at the passers-by.

The meat locker in Father's shop filled with small headless birds.
We eat Cornish hens and Mother cries for no apparent reason.

HIS LAST WORDS

Before they wheel my father
into the operating room
for emergency heart surgery
I ask if he wants to see
new pictures of my one-year-old.
His *No* stings for a second and then
he asks about my new book.
Go through my mail please
to see if my cousin Gretl
from Haifa ordered a copy
as though it were a salami or
a pound of cold cuts from his store.
Until that moment I thought
my father could never know me—
that it was his fault.

THE MACHINE

1.

In Mother's room the breathing machine doesn't stop.
Listening, I try to learn a lesson about love.
I'll use it as long as it works—
her concession to me because she would like to be done
with it, the three-month prognosis an eternity to her.
When Mother was about to give birth to me
the doctor was late so the nurse yelled at her
to stop pushing and keep her legs together.
Now I imagine being in that half-state—
Mother ready to release me: a room of first breaths.

2.

When they pick up the machine Mother apologizes.
She wonders if she's disappointing me by not fighting,
the disease so rampant she can barely move.
When I try to feed her she reminds me of the times
she fed me, each spoonful for a family member.
She says they were so worried when I stopped eating.
In Germany they would have pinched my nose to force
my mouth open. That's what they did to my uncle Norman.
So why didn't you eat, she laughs, *was life so bad?*
It's dusk: the room is quiet when she pushes away my arm.

GAME BOARD

Mother knows her time is near
when she can no longer move her hands
to place the Scrabble tiles.
She asks for my help—
I lay down her letters so each one
fits perfectly in the small boxes, confirming
with each click the tiles are lined up.
The word is *season*, Mother reluctant
as ever to use two esses in one word.
H-E-L-P she whispers,
each letter stuck in her throat,
unsure whether to swallow or spit it out.
It's early evening—dusk
in collusion with remaining light.

Green Balloons

Mother on her deathbed tells me she's ready
to move to California. She can hardly turn
to face me and her body is so light I imagine
she could float out the window and ascend
above Manhattan. There, the building where
I grew up—the graffitied elevator
Mother painted because it was the one thing
that set us apart from surrounding walk-ups.
Fifth Avenue—it's 1939, St. Patrick's Day
and she's just off the boat from Germany
thinking this parade *must* be for us.
Her father is on the sidelines in tears and she says
to herself *Wir können jetzt glücklich sein*
but he never stops crying.

Mother's eyes are closed as I hold her in
morphine sleep whispering *Sure, you can move now.*
Below her a sea of green balloons
that gives way to hills joined by a slender bridge.
She hears my children yelling *Grandma,*
come down, read us a story in German
but she can't land, their words ballast for the living.

MOTHER WANTS TO KNOW

Mother in the clothes shop wants to know
how a red dress looks on her,
Your father will say no one notices me anyway.
Mother in the kitchen wants to know
how she could've married a man so stupid,
I was always the good girl, did what I was told.
Mother in the living room wants to know
how she'll ever find a job,
My parents didn't let me finish high school.

Mother at the pediatrician's wants to know
why I get sick so often,
Do you want to give me a heart attack?
Mother in the museum wants to know
how the Holocaust could have affected me,
Ich bin froh das ich hier bin.
Mother in my bedroom wants to know
why I keep writing,
It's not about me I hope.

Mother in my apartment wants to know
when I'll settle down,
Some marriages work out just fine.
Mother at my house wants to know
if we'll name the baby after my father,
He had a few good traits you know.
Mother in a wheelchair wants to know
if I'll help her end her life, if not
I can still roll myself to the window.

Mother on her deathbed wants to know
if I'll lie down beside her,
Here, in the spot where your father slept.

The Turning

A day before Mother dies
she calls out Father's name—
the long version, *Maximilian*.
It comes out like a question as if
she is asking whether or not
he will embrace her after the years
she has been alone trying
to come into her own name, Flora—
a calla lily, gracious but still mournful.
Or after all the times she screamed at him
and called him *Idiot*,
even in front of the neighbors,
the three syllables that would ring
through our tiny apartment,
putting us on alert: Mother is depressed.
Towards the end when she watched TV
she wanted me to fix the characters'
marital problems, her way perhaps
of asking forgiveness. She would turn to me
especially during the screaming and beg:
Please, please, you have to help them.

THE UNDERTAKER

It's early Sunday morning and I bolted out of sleep two hours ago—the silence harsh, unforgiving. Time hasn't moved, the apartment sealed in near-perfect stillness as we take our new roles—Mother triumphant, after an illness she could only beat by dying quickly, and I'm left to cheer her on.

When the undertaker arrives, I'm still unkempt and wearing pajamas: white logo T-shirt, gray silk bottoms with diamond stripes. He follows the design up my legs until I interrupt to tell him where the body is. He checks for signs of life then uncovers Mother, and I imagine the autopsy—the pink nightgown cut down the middle revealing her previous disease, one breast still a scar.

The undertaker tells me this is his first case of the day, then wants to know more about me. *Oh San Francisco* he says, smiling, his eyes searching mine, then he's back with the morning events: he'll put Mother in a bag, place her on the gurney, then take her down the freight elevator to avoid the neighbors. He'll transport her to the hospital for the autopsy, then pick her up to take her to the funeral home. When I see her in the morning she'll look as good as she does now. *Well, better. Like a bride.*

He walks to the foot of the bed to put a tag on Mother's toe, then walks to the top to pull off her rings. *The diamond, isn't it beautiful* he says, placing the rings on my palm and holding them there.

LAST WORDS

And when we die, everything is open again.
Open closed open. That's all we are.
—from *Open Closed Open*, by Yehuda Amichai
(as translated by Chana Bloch and Chana Kronfeld)

The only plan I made before Mother died
was what I would read at her funeral—
a section of Rilke's *Duino Elegies*,
a few lines by Amichai.
Mother would have preferred prose, a few words
about being a refugee from Hitler's Germany,
the job she landed at the Federal Reserve Bank—
22 years of outstanding performance evaluations
still filed under 'F' in her accordion folder.
She always found poetry incomprehensible
not unlike her body at my side,
nothing more than a string of nouns—
head, neck, shoulder, arms, hands.
When I'm asked to identify the body again
all I can muster is the word *yes*
and the man in black accepts it.
He closes the slat in the coffin
next to Mother's face and I begin to read.

ENCOUNTER

I glimpse at a mirror, the rendezvous always surprising.
A bodhisattva wanders the earth, eyes in his hands.

Father comes to my poetry reading after taking the subway,
   a cross-town bus.
Isaac can no longer tell the difference between outrage
   and humility.

Mother on her deathbed, my sister won't hold her hand.
The sheets are lifted off the mirrors: eclipse of the soul.

The photo double-exposed, two men peer into each other.
In *The Boxer,* Bonnard rages against his double.

A dream: my reflection in the eyes of a tiger.
In the *Torah.* when God gets angry, his nostrils flare.

STATEMENT RECORDING THE PROPERTY OF JEWS

Each calculation rounded to the highest Mark.
First the assets: the kosher meat market and apartment
at Zeil 51 in Frankfurt on June 28, 1938,
the money in the bank, life insurance, watch and chain,
small allotment for furnishings. Then the liabilities:
deductions for personal debt at 5.5, 6, 8.5%,
money owed by three siblings who had already fled.
Grandfather's signature is bold, florid—
a man going through the motions, someone who believes
the Nazis will come to their senses.
My grandparents had left the meat market early that day,
gone upstairs to change and tell the nanny what to prepare
for dinner—*Kalbsbraten, Spätzle*, a green salad.
Grandfather wears his best suit, Grandmother a silk blouse,
long skirt, fitted jacket, felt down brim hat.
On the way to the Gestapo, Grandmother suggests
they rehearse—*Tell them my sister in New York*
will put up the bond, offer them the gold watch—
but Grandfather has none of it. They walk
arm in arm, heads pointed in different directions,
the ostrich feather in Grandmother's hat
askew, just reaching her husband's chin.

SHADOW

In the letter from the Holocaust Commission
they are pleased to offer me an award.
My grandparents are dead. My parents.
I shake the envelope: photos spill out.
First two, then four, twenty, fifty, a hundred.
I pick up one, a distant aunt—
the high forehead, light eyebrows, thin lips.
She stares off to the side, a shadow
like bat's wings hovering in a corner.
A small pulse in her neck gets stronger
then the photos begin to rise, faces
folding, unfolding around the room.

ARTIFACT

1.

Winding up grandfather's *tefillin*
to send to Berlin's Jewish Museum,
I see him unraveling the straps
in his farmhouse kitchen in Germany
then binding his arm and head:
I will betroth you unto Me forever.
When the Gestapo comes
he wraps the *tefillin* tightly,
almost enough to stop
the rhythm of his heart.

2.

Grandfather on display
in the country he fled:
tefillin without an arm or head
but a voice that still pleads
And you shall know the Lord.
A man hears it and takes a photo—
his reflection captured in glass.

HUBERT, 1990

I visit Dachau with a German friend
and decide this will begin my reconciliation
after growing up with stories about
my grandfather's internment in this camp—
his notes home begging for butter because
it's supposed to ease the nerves—
the understanding my sister and I
could want for nothing.
Then Hubert tells me he grew up
never learning about the camps—even
his mother living nearby said nothing.
Now when he confronts her she's angry:
Wir haben von nichts gewusst.
He asked her about the trains,
the pounding boxcars and she thought
Germany was moving men to the front.
He says *Too bad our country is unified again.*
Outside snow on the ground:
not one boot print.

DAS RHEINGOLD

When the Gestapo was rounding up the Jews, they only let them take
musical instruments if they could prove they could play them.
—David Akov, Consulate General of Israel, in a speech
commemorating *Yom Hashoah*, 2008

A ten-year-old boy plays *Für Elise* on the piano.
Mother whimpers and the officer tells her to shut up.
He yells at the boy to slow down,
Beethoven wrote a love song, not a piece for runners.
Now he wants Wagner, *Das Rheingold*,
assuming the boy won't be able to play it
so he can be done with this nonsense
and take the piano home to his children,
hire Frau Schmidt to give lessons.
He's surprised when he hears the long E-flat
and imagines the bassoons, then the horns and soon
the three Rhine maidens, guardians of the river's gold.
The boy misses a note and the officer tells him
to start again, to slow down, speed up.
He smacks him in the head when Alberich
renounces love for power and storms out
with the other SS, yelling the family has one day
to pack their belongings and get the hell out.

The Golem

Every December Eddie the barber
tells me about his Jewish friend Mark
who buys a Hanukkah bush,
decorates it with lights,
stars of David made from foil.
He hates being Jewish—
even had a nose job and now
he looks like Miss Piggy.

I imagine Mark at the plastic surgeon's
going through a catalog of faces
and choosing the one with the smallest nose.
Moments before surgery
the doctor has a revelation:
he wants to turn him into a beautiful man,
someone who will open doors, turn heads.
Why not make them spin?

Midrash

Moses addresses God as though He were a man.
During my Bar Mitzvah, the stammer stops.

Cain is blinded by his love of Abel.
My sister breaks my favorite LP: *Bird Dogs* fall from the sky.

Noah saves a pair from each species.
Mother has an idea: the two of us against the world.

The last time God was revealed to a human: the prophet Samuel.
Grandfather ensures his family the *Heimat* will be saved.

Moses never reaches the promised land.
Father returns to his German hometown but I refuse to go.

2

There are more things in heaven and earth, Horatio,
Than are dreamt of in your philosophy.
But come:
Here as before, never, so help you mercy.

—from *Hamlet*, by William Shakespeare

THE LAST SIGNS OF THE BOURGEOISIE

after the painting, *The Floor Scrapers,*
by Caillebotte, 1876

Standing on a stepladder he instructs the workers
to scrape away the shellacked floors that held
the baby grand, an overstuffed couch where
the bankers reminisced about the Franco-Prussian war,
a marble table that held snifters with fingers of Courvoisier.
He's surprised by how easily the finish peels off
reminding him of the days after sunburn,
the pale young woman who lived here
with her husband and was reluctant to sell the flat
to a painter who would turn it into his studio.
She could sense him mock the chandeliers,
the small Degas, the Baccarat crystal—
a man of means who would have it both ways.
He made just the right offer, pleased
he was irritating her and making it worse
by praising the couple's move to Honfleur—
the water would no doubt be good for her nerves—
at which she stormed out, petticoats sweeping
the light now being scraped from the floor
and he'll salvage for his paintings.
He closes his eyes and imagines his work on the walls—
yes, he'll consider a painting of the floor scrapers,
their bodies intent on reclaiming the room.

FREE FALL

Our last night in Europe,
a fair in Brussels
just for us—
scent of waffles,
whipped cream,
strawberries.
We ride the Ferris wheel,
the worst part going up
because we anticipate
the ride down:
arriving in New York,
our little cage
swinging, the operator
holding it steady
as he opens the door
on one side,
then the other
and each of us
steps out
into a separating
night.

EDGE

Swimming side-by-side we lose all sense of boundaries.
Letters mingle in the air: a flock of crows rehearsing my words.

Mother confides in me—a boy the size of an ear.
Father at the dinner table: sound of steak being masticated.

I'm sleeping in the living room of the old apartment and hear a
    window shatter.
For Isaac it starts off as an ordinary day.

Michelangelo's *Captives* try to break free from the stone.
You hook your arm into mine and we vanish.

Refugees from Darfur flee across the border to Chad.
First came the Big Bang, then God.

CROSSING

When we see them from the road to Essouria we're stunned
even though we were told to expect them: the goats
grazing in the branches of the Argan trees.
It seems like a dream and minutes later we laugh
and talk about it that way—the black shapes
symbols of a darker side gone wild. And then
what it would be like to live in Morocco together—
the unfamiliar freeing us, the border
between what we do and don't know thinning.

Mornings we walk through the medina, arms locked
then return to our tiny room with a bed and sink,
where the rushing sounds of the hall toilet
drown out the muezzin, the net
over our bed becoming second skin.
In the desert the dunes appear like waves
and you say you'll sculpt them that way—
the white marble undulating in the light.

THE DECISION

after the painting, *A Lady Writing,*
by Johannes Vermeer, c1665

It appears the light is emanating
from the letter itself so the woman
must have reached her decision, in fact
she's so intent she can't lift the pen
from the paper as she glances
up at the artist, eyes aglow,
lips turned into a small smile
as if to say she'll accept
the pearls lying on the table:
from every corner of her eyes, yes, yes,
her feather pen about to float
out of her hand, into the source of light.

SISTERS

Teaching my two-year-old to swim,
pudgy arms dog paddling
across the baby pool,
head lifted to keep it
from getting splashed.
I turn to watch
my five-year-old swim, her
hey dad, watch me,
an expected tap on the shoulder,
arms now attempting freestyle,
legs like drumsticks
be-bopping the pool.
I tell her to keep her head down
then turn back to my two-year-old:
she's lying face up
under the water,
eyes wide open,
her body suspended.
My hands slice through the pool,
swing her up—
arc of joy that belies relief:
a voiceless *be-bop,*
be-bop approaches.

With My Mother and Five-Year-Old at Disneyworld

Even as a grandmother she's completely unsure
worrying as ever about whether or not
my daughter is wearing enough sunscreen
or what would happen if she got lost.
My mother wants to buy her everything in sight—
Beauty and the Beast socks, Minnie Mouse watch—
but even my daughter realizes something is wrong
when she laughs to her mom on the phone,
Grandma wants to buy me everything
and then moments later,
I know grandmas are for more than shopping.
One morning when they are by themselves
I see them revolve through the lobby door,
first my mother who stops when she gets outside,
peers in all directions and then my daughter
skipping, her pony tail bouncing behind her:
Grandma, I'll show you which way to go.
This way, this way. Follow me.

FEAR

When my six-year-old
throws a ball
and it hits
an antique brandy bottle
on the mantle
she lets out a wail
even before
I can reprimand her—
this knowing
before knowing
that makes me
rush over to hold her,
the two of us
surrounded by
shattered glass,
in tears.

Viewing Art

My eight-year-old
is admiring Brancusi,
says he's exotic,
the way he put together
a bird
from pieces of wood
and now it looks
like it could soar.
When we leave
the Modern
she doesn't notice
the sparrows
as they take flight:
small words with wings.

BOWLING AT GRAND LANES

Just the sight of the man's ball
weighs me down—
it's heavy, black, and glows.
Still he drops it into the polisher
and watches his girlfriend
as she places her red one on the carousel.
She's white tank-top, pink shorts,
curly blond hair in an upswept pony tail.
He picks up his ball and throws it
like a softball: his arm extends sideways
and it looks as though the ball will land
in the fourth lane over but it drops
perfectly into his lane, a bit off course
then straightens out to become a strike.
Each time he does this the woman jumps
into his arms and they make out
as the black and red balls collide
coming out of the chute—his score
after three frames, higher than mine after six.

In our lane my children toss bowling balls
as though they are boulders.
Each one lands with a thud
and as it creeps down the lane
my kids jump up and down yelling
way to go with thumbs up even though
the ball mostly stops just short of the pins.

TEACHING POETRY IN HIGH SCHOOL

The boys don't know what to make of me.
I'm the last period of the day,
the obstacle between them and basketball
or an afternoon playing *World of Warcraft*.
A boy in the back hesitates, raises his hand.
I assume he'll ask to go to the bathroom
and the other boys will chuckle but
he wants to read his poem, the one
I assigned based on a painting by Hopper—
a couple in a room alone,
the man reading a newspaper,
the woman playing piano with two fingers.
The boy imagines she's playing
Chopsticks to count the time:
She made a few mistakes
but he didn't notice.
Till death do them part.
So she kept on playing her tune.

The boy doesn't look up as the bell rings—
he kicks a mote of dust as he leaves the room.

In the Sauna

I'm invisible as the 17-year-old boys strut in
after admiring their small tattoos in the mirror,
each one carefully placed on a shoulder—
a sideways 69, fire-breathing dragon, rose, two hearts.
Their talk moves from high-school lacrosse to girls
and my heart races when I recognize one of the boys
as my daughter's friend. I can't decide
if I should greet him so I make sure I'm
well-hidden behind the *New York Times Book Review*
as they talk about the latest hot thing,
who is doing what to whom when Rachel's parents
take off weekends for their home in the Sierras.
I flip the pages noisily, not reading one word
until the discussion shifts to baseball and for once
I'm grateful for our national pastime:
The fucking A's, dudes, what do you think
of those fucking, fucking A's.

LETTER FROM SIENA

Suor Celeste writes to her father about
the storm in Arcetri that wreaked havoc
on his home and whether or not she should replace
the terra cotta pot that held the orange tree.
Galileo considers every word so when he writes back
to tell her to keep the orange tree planted in the ground,
perhaps it will grow and yield fruit,
he mentions he is also trying to heal.
Try as he may he can only imagine the earth
as the center of the universe and
what a happy thought that is, not unlike
his faith in God that keeps him sane here in Siena
where the stars are often so bright they seem to confirm
everything that will remain hidden around them.

THE BUILDER

He knows the places where you like to hang mirrors,
the way you stand in a shower to make sure
the water hits you at just the right angle,
the thin lining of your bank account.
When you bring up the virtues of *Feng Shui*
he rolls his eyes wondering if you're trying
to convert him to a new religion.
He knocks on the walls that separate lives
and as he points out the ones made of lath and plaster
you imagine them crumbling during a tremor,
secrets bathing the house in a quiet glow.
When he tells you to tear down ceilings,
move walls and rooms, chances are
he'll have your ear for just a few moments,
your world reduced to an erector set:
the simplicity of starting over again and again.

Demolishing a Log Cabin: Headquarters, Kentucky

In the kitchen we tear off layers of wallpaper—
rows of tulips, columns of roses and daisies—
and then I see a note: *Jane loves Billy, May 1942.*
This must be her testimony: they've been going steady
for years and decide to get engaged before Billy
goes off to war. The evening before he leaves
Billy is more insistent than ever,
the *what if* hovering in the car
where he kisses her breasts and touches her.

When he drops her off she heads straight
to her room, her face a reluctant glow.
She's not sure if she's angry at Billy,
if she should weep or confess to her diary
so she tosses and turns, touches herself to smell
and taste him. At first she's repulsed,
the scent of salt and blood, and then she remembers
what Billy felt like, his desire, not just for her
but for something outside their bodies.
She goes back downstairs for a glass of milk,
wanders through the kitchen touching stray objects—
a cooking spoon, ladle—and picks up the pencil.

Mr. Barnes

At the end of a gravel path, rural Kentucky,
a small farmer, mustache mouth, straggly white beard,
rounds up an old horse he believes is his.
Mind standin' in the middle 'a the path there?
Gotta try to corner'im.
When I make my move the horse lurches,
cuts a wide swath around me, then gallops into the hills.
I think that horse's mine but I'm not sure.
Got those white markings.
I live over the fence there.
Been there 30 years and haven't left the area.
None 'a my horses ever cut loose either.
Got six, they're best friends.
One leaves and the other starts cryin' like a baby.
Do you hear a horse cryin'?

Walking on I think of an interview I just read,
a Dutch painter saying he doesn't travel much now:
the more people travel, the less they have to say.

VIGIL: FINISHING THE BARN

Sinar and I are hanging drywall, taking turns
holding up the ceiling and drilling in the screws.
His girlfriend and baby son are now due in Kentucky
tomorrow—same story every day this week.
Supposed to be traveling from Houston
on a bus run by Mexicans because
they know how to avoid *La Migra*.
She's young, scared to leave her family
but he says he's ready to settle down
(*¡No he visto a mi bebé en cuatro meses!*)
Sinar isn't sure how many kids he has,
three or four he thinks, one in Guatemala and
the rest in Mexico—but they're all girls.
Cada niño necesita a su papá.
Next week Sinar will tape the drywall—
the tattoo of Jesus Christ on his bicep
flexing and contracting as he waits for his son.

THE LAUNDRESS AND HER SON

after the painting, *The Laundress*,
by Jean-Baptiste-Simeon Chardin, 1733

The laundress is startled, riveted by the sound of a rat
that might be scurrying through the cellar
and find her son blowing bubbles beside the wash barrel.
Or she is struck by the sudden light
and the shadow of the man walking through it,
his gait so similar to her last master's.
She had noticed him watching her but didn't understand
until he came up from behind while she was ironing
and simply hiked up her skirt, helping himself
as he did to everything else in the house—the way
he would just stick his fingers into the crème fraiche,
or consume the éclairs, brulee, the Courvoisier.
She was never taken by his words but
by the sound of his voice, the warm breath that filled her
from one evening to the next—until she was asked
one day to leave at once: the boy now eight
and dusk settling on the Rue de Chalon,
the cold air rushing in through a crack in the window.

Elevator Down to the 'A' Train

The doors open onto a scene by Bonnard:
photos of babies and cats cover the elevator walls,
a plastic fern and fuchsia hang from the ceiling
and a fake Persian mat is in the corner where the operator
sits on a stool listening to a fugue by Bach.
She pulls the handle to shut the door
and the people become quiet, almost reverent
as they step from photo to photo—
the operator and baby at a birthday party,
the baby holding a calico kitten—
and a few of the riders start to chat:
the resemblance between the operator and baby,
the two of them sitting under an umbrella
that has to be on the south end of Jones Beach
(*and boy was it hot there this weekend*),
an older woman who must be the baby's grandmother.
The subway noise begins to drown out Bach,
the elevator comes to a slow halt and everyone
becomes silent again as they shuffle toward
the operator and hover around the door,
waiting for her to pull the handle the other way.

The Carpool

The code of silence is taken so seriously
no passenger dares to sneeze.
In the next lane, windows wide open
a Hispanic man is wailing a song,
the round *O* of his mouth
caressing the word *amor*.
Our eyes meet and he looks puzzled—
he points at the clear morning sky
and continuing the gesture
he waves his arm like a conductor,
the cars stopping and starting
to the beat of his song.

CELL PHONE

The woman on the packed bus is sure
all of us are interested in her latest shopping spree
(lingerie at half price, silk blouses a steal),
how much she loved the new Woody Allen movie,
the awful dinner party she attended the night before.
When I tap her shoulder to tell her
we've heard enough she turns around
but doesn't see me. Perhaps she thinks
someone is encouraging her to tell us more
so she calls her boyfriend and tells him
no, it was all her fault
but maybe it's time to call things off.
Novels begin to close, newspapers fold
as her words circulate through the bus,
all of us now the boyfriend
eager to acknowledge a dread of commitment.

Virginia Woolf in San Francisco, 2008

Surely she would be shocked by the lack of propriety—
just the thought of a woman marrying a woman
might be enough to topple the imagination,
cause her to stop writing for months
after which she would begin a letter to Vita:
The light here is so penetrating
it seems to make everything transparent...
Words take wing, aimed straight for the heart.

She would take the hills in long strides
wondering if it might not be too demanding
trying to match one's mood to this much light.
Sussex is so dreary it's easy to turn to Leonard
and talk about the weather as though the psyche,
the dark clouds so ominous one doesn't want to attempt
anything too ambitious—a hike through the forest,
even the thought of taking pen to paper.

Over time she might feel comforted to discover
how little life has changed: marriage so engrained
that two women would even consider it,
a public so foolish they have turned her into an icon
for feminism of all things
when all she had wanted was to blur the lines,
Leonard and Vita each holding one of her hands
as they walk wordlessly across the downs.

MID-FIFTIES MAN

Mid-fifties man. *Recently discovered guilt. Can't wait to try it out.*
Box no. 7297.
—*The London Review of Books* (classified ad)

The lies would be unstoppable.
Our discussion about the latest Martin Amis
was so titillating I got distracted during sex
even though you are the best lover in the world.
He meets a woman skiing in Bulgaria
and tells her his wife just divorced him
so now he has custody of their anorexic daughter,
two standard poodles with epilepsy.
The woman's arms encircle him all night
allowing him to drift off beyond the Moussala slopes
to his small flat in Hampstead Heath,
the Booker short list stacked in size and color order
on his nightstand, bindings facing out
alongside a cup drained of its pekoe tea:
an orange ring now holding the moonlight.

DOG AT THE DINING TABLE

after the painting, *Woman with Dog*,
by Pierre Bonnard, 1922

The woman's husband prepared her favorite meal—
duck, wild rice, asparagus—after giving her the news
about his unexpected trip to the south of France,
another meeting with an art dealer
although she still suspects a mistress
and searches for clues as soon as he arrives home—
scent of perfume, strands of dark hair.
The dog is sympathetic to the woman's sadness
as it sits quietly on her lap, easy this evening
after the long walk in the *Bois de Boulogne* where it chased
the same squirrel from one oak tree to the next.
Throughout the meal the dog doesn't budge but now—
the smell of the Port Salut a cue—
the dog will jump off the woman's lap,
head straight for the garden and dive
into a patch of lawn that is soft and wet
and every blade smells unequivocally of the earth.

Exposed

Overheard on the bus, a woman leaves a message:
I hope it's OK to leave you a personal voicemail at work,
the cancer is back, god help me.

. . . . . .

A sweet pea climbs up the face
of an apartment building,
its buds, like tiny feet, determined.

. . . . . .

My father is invited back to his German village—
a parade for him through town and then he's taken to his home,
once confiscated by the same crowd.

. . . . . .

Next door our neighbors are singing in
Hebrew, *Grace after Meals*: the fog lifts,
the stars assemble in a single word—Amen.

. . . . . .

At Pt. Reyes we decide to veer off the trail:
after love, you pull up a dandelion and blow—
the white seeds fly past in a grand finale.

. . . . . .

Sea water enters the tide pool:
the starfish stirs, an anemone opens its lips,
a hermit crab attempts the getaway.

UNDERTOW

Madame Butterfly renounces everything for her lover.
Your breath was always a phone call away.

On a church billboard, *Love is not a feeling, but a choice.*
We can still be friends you say, friends who make love.

My wife, stuck in an undertow, cries for help.
The water breaks: my newborn rushes out.

I push a pencil through one of the support beams of our home.
My wife prunes back the abutilon: pile of red bells.

A rising tide, the anemone opens its lips.
We feel the rising tide and let go.

3

Leaning over this parapet I see far out a waste of water. A fin turns. This bare visual impression is unattached to any line of reason, it springs up as one might see the fin of a porpoise on the horizon.

—from *The Waves,* by Virginia Woolf

CONCERT

I'm walking down Second
working on a poem
when I spot him sitting
on the corner of Stillman
conducting an orchestra.
His arms sway back and forth
and I imagine musicians playing
Rachmaninoff's *Concerto Number 2 in C Minor.*
I can hear the piano and
when he points
the violins, then the horns.
The music gets louder
as his arms get more animated—
Rachmaninoff's triumph over doubt—
the crescendo drowning out the traffic,
the endless noise of words.

MATINEE

after the painting, *The Balcony*,
by Edward Hopper, 1928

This is her weekly trip to the cinema,
the only time she likes to be alone.
When she wakes up Thursday mornings,
her husband already gone, she puts on a dress, hat,
comfortable heels and boards a trolley for the noon show.
When the theatre darkens, her mood lifts:
she can forget the apartment that needs fresh paint,
her mother who sends letters twice a week about home,
always ending with a few lines about how darling
Mary's grandchildren are and she can't wait to have her turn.
The woman gives a passing thought to her husband,
how hard he works, but she's not sure why he has to work late
two nights a week, so late that he often has to stay in town
because he misses the last trolley home.
When she lets her mind wander she stops at the middle office,
the number of secretaries dizzying,
most so young they might be fresh out of high school.
The theatre is dark now and the newsreel starts:
The Discovery of Penicillin Changes the World.
Earhart Becomes the First Woman to Fly the Atlantic.
She saw the same clip about Earhart last week and it's still
unimaginable: a woman climbing up the steps to the plane,
turning around to wave at the crowd and stepping into the dark
cockpit as the propellers begin to whir, the noise drowning out
the voices, the people of Newfoundland cheering her on.

Testifying Before the Judiciary Committee

How do I talk about grace
to a panel of strangers
representing thousands
whose interests must be served—
the final moments when those
who can no longer move
are endowed with wings
and want to home in
on the place they once knew
and know for a first time, its radiance.
A tiny bone moves through my throat—
still I try words like *paralysis, respirator*.
I mention the silence that can only be
broken by blinking the eyes.
Three blinks means *enough*.
Someone gasps, then
the man on the top bench,
the one in the middle holding the mike,
is tracking a small black bird
that appears in the room.

ONE BY ONE

A man on trial for indecent exposure
and one by one, potential jurors
explain why they cannot serve.
The woman raped at gunpoint
shows us her scar,
a tiny bird with three wings
trapped on her neck.
Another woman recounts the footsteps
following her in the snow,
the hand on her mouth pulling her down,
her muffled screams
quieting the courtroom.
A man describes a stranger's big fist
clutching his genitals, the promise
of candy on a Manhattan rooftop.
The defense tries euphemisms,
penis, masturbation
but some of us see a hooded face,
the shiny edge of a knife,
or candy bars floating above a building
and they're just beyond our grasp.

Phone Bank: The Olympic Torch

Some have a hard time understanding this relay:
San Francisco, Beijing, Darfur.
I explain—the oil, arms sales, close to a half million lives.
Others say the Olympics have nothing to do
with politics or with China.
One man can't be bothered and I want to assure him
I won't be asking for money but he hangs up.
I imagine he's watching TV,
hopefully the news, hopefully the image of
the Darfurian girl in the desert, her torn blanket
shelter from a sandstorm but chances are
he's riveted to a crime show—
a 14-year-old raped by her stepfather
but the wife claims the girl is not the victim.
She provoked it, she says,
pointing a finger at the girl, *she provoked it*.

CONJUNCTION

Exxon Mobil has profits of $8 billion in one quarter.
A woman living on Folsom wants to teach me how to fly.

On the café radio, the story of a girl being raped in Darfur.
The score from last night's Giants game implodes.

Says a poet, *to live is to do evil*.
I climb a mountain and won't stop until I glimpse heaven.

The closer we are to Sinai, the closer we are to the truth.
In my daughter's Midrash, God as talisman.

Another car bomb in Baghdad.
A new device controls your TV from anywhere in the world.

The Anatomy Lesson

after the painting, *The Anatomy Lesson of Dr. Tulp*,
by Rembrandt, 1632

The doctor usually begins his lesson with the intestines—
the ileocecal valve like the lock of a canal—
but Rembrandt spares the viewer
and focuses instead on the arm and hand,
the parts that perform surgery, hold a palette,
push back a strand of hair from the beloved's face.
The students turn to the doctor as he extols
the miracle of the human body—morality
hardly a science, the cadaver once a petty thief
who tried to steal a nobleman's cape.
With that the doctor turns away.
Perhaps he hears the music that caught his ear
the day before walking past the Oude Kerk,
Sweelinck on the harpsichord,
his notes keeping time with a light summer rain.

TRUE NORTH

Across from me in an airport lounge
a man draws me as I write poetry.
I find shelter imagining what I might be:
line drawing, life-like portrait,
or Francis Bacon man, eyes askew,
glasses lowered on a misshapen nose.
He places me in a high-back chair,
the light from the study window
reflecting on my manuscript, a novel
set in nineteenth-century France.
When our departure is announced
the man notes changes he'll make
when we arrive in his TriBeCa loft
and then he folds me away,
looking past me as he boards the plane.

VOYAGE

The plane is dark except for one light in the galley
where a stewardess chips away at a block of ice.
She would be embarrassed if she knew
I notice how intent she is,
that I might go so far as imagining
what's on her mind—the ice giving way to
a face, a hand, a man's torso.
Or perhaps she's thinking of a phone call
unanswered on the other side of the world.
Today I'll be alone in a city where no one knows me.
It's my weakness, to enjoy being invisible
on a crowded street where I can't understand the words.
When I can take a walk on the *Ile St. Louis*,
look into a window and join the family for a lunch
of rabbit or fish, a glass of Bordeaux,
grandfather rambling on about life under de Gaulle—
until someone knocks into me, and I vanish.

THE FLAT-FOOTED AMERICAN

At *Tianhe Zuliao* Reflexology a young woman
brings me a bucket of steaming herbal water,
infusion of eucalyptus and jasmine.
I'm reclined, Birkenstocks off revealing
my flat feet, the cause of the *plantar fasciitis*
that makes me wince if I don't stretch after running.
The woman returns in ten minutes and cradles
each foot in her arm as she dries it and then
kneads all the tiny bones, forgiving the steps
I've taken since arriving in Beijing:
the hot morning runs through the *hutong*
where people stop when they see me then carry on
once they recognize another Caucasian;
the strolls through Tiananmen Square,
prey for hawkers who want to sell me wrist watches
with Mao's smiling image, his arm the second hand
that waves at me as the moments pass.
When she presses one point I jump. *Stomach OK?*
I list a litany of digestive problems, expecting sympathy
for my lactose intolerance but she can only smile back,
her eyes tiny jade Buddhas. *Forbidden City?*
I nod recalling how concubines entertained
the Qing emperors, the inner courts where I imagine
they began by massaging the feet.

SNAPSHOT: XI'AN, 2005

After visiting the old couple who lives in a cave
in the mountains outside Xi'an I see the sign:
The civilized and tidy circumstance is a kind of enjoyment.
I assume it's notice for tourists to be respectful
of the monuments but then I recall the giant poster
of Mao still hanging over the couple's only table.
He has a big smile and the couple is happy
to pose in front of him, the man
pulling out his blue cap with the red star
and placing it on his head, eyes rolling up
to make sure the brim is perfectly centered.

Tito's Batons

In Tito's Monument
hundreds of youth relay batons—
gifts from the children of Yugoslavia
in the shapes of missiles, torpedoes, grenades.
I imagine the annual competition—
the creator of the most threatening baton wins—
then it is handed off from athlete to athlete,
city to city: from Ljubljana to Zagreb,
Zagreb to Dubrovnik, Dubrovnik to Sarajevo...
Now they surround Titos' remains
and I think he would be pleased—
the batons protecting him in death as in life—
even though my wife and I are the only ones
at the monument, camera hidden and on.

VERDICT

On a flight from Belgrade to Ljubljana
a woman tells me it's all the Americans' fault—
the situation in Kosovo,
long lines at the airport,
rising price of oil.
Over Bosnia she lets on
she is Serbian yet despised Milosevic
and then *Aren't we all victims?*
I recall the Annie Liebovitz photo:
the fallen bicycle in Sarajevo—
the teen killed by a sniper,
his books still strapped to the back seat,
the circle of fresh blood.

Unfinished

It's 2 AM, the cafés along the *Ljubljanica*
are full and the laughter
enters my sleepless night: I'm 23,
back on the houseboat in Amsterdam.
We're having a party but I decide to go
to my room, write to a friend—
I won't be coming home anytime soon.
I'm at my desk that's covered—
books, journals, paper—and look up:
a fire is raging across the canal.

OPATIYA

Early Sunday morning on *Lungomare*
an old couple wades into the sea holding hands.
The man dives in and breaks into freestyle,
the woman steadies herself on small rocks.
The man turns around and they wave,
their arms reaching over a generation
or a year. It hardly matters
now that they've come to this time
outside of time—the sun just having risen,
the city still braced in sleep
as the church bell resounds seven times
then is silenced by water reaching shore.

WOMAN PLAYING THE THEORBO

after the painting, *The Music Lesson,*
by Gerard Terborch, c1670

Perhaps he's not her music master after all
even though he taps the baton on the stand quickly
to encourage her to pick up the pace.
He's an older man, a friend of the family
and her parents make the introduction
hoping he'll find her attractive, the girl nineteen
and already approaching her prime.
She's told to play *Vespers* for the gentleman,
a member of the guild and an accomplished cellist
who commissioned a self-portrait by Hals.
She tries to refuse but her father will not hear of it.
The man taps the baton on the stand impatiently now
the same way he'll tap his knife on the long
dining room table complaining about the servants
who serve the *hutspot* too cold or too hot,
or about his wife who should be dressing the children
in warmer clothing with ice already on the canals.
She'll nod even though she'll be hearing music:
the piece she played the afternoon of his first visit
only this time she hears it slowly,
the way Claudio Monteverdi intended.

Mt. Ste. Victoire

Viewing Cezanne's *Mt. Ste. Victoire* we talk about
our hikes on that mountain—a backpack with
baguette, *Laughing Cow*, bottle of Bordeaux,
stories about your landlady, a widow
who rationed water in case there was another war,
reports from our high school friends
who insisted we find the latest Grateful Dead LP.
It was just after college, you were living in Aix
and I, in Amsterdam, and we were determined
to keep our options open. That's what we wrote home:
We're living in Europe and keeping our options open—
no marriages like our parents', the yelling and flash silences,
no desk jobs where people smoke Newports,
the menthol rings, lozenges that would make us choke.
Those were our concerns as we walked in and out
of the light, the borders between us diminishing
like the hills in the painting by Cezanne
where we pause now and talk about our families—
daughters leaving home, our restive lives.

AFTER WE DECIDE TO WORK THINGS OUT

I sit in the backyard reading,
the language on the page
easier to follow than our voices,
a tumult of words.
It's a poem about how we fight against
inevitability and then the inevitable changes—
what's left are the things that matter:
a touch on the shoulder,
smell of basil in the garden,
the words we share for beauty—
gladiola, abutilon, alstroemeria.

You bring out a bottle of champagne,
small dish of almonds and sit down beside me.
Wordless, we stare at the rising bubbles—
sentence of tiny pearls.

TUG-OF-WAR

The girl wants her parents to disappear
so she thunders back to her room and
begins to set boundaries: music turned up,
floor strewn with underwear, jeans,
T-shirts, colorful scarves with beads—
a room inhabited by clothing without a body.

Father in the living room is culling
history from the *New York Times*. The tension
in the house is measured by the snap of each page,
but it's nothing compared to the violence in
Afghanistan, the U.S. like other invaders
failing to save the people from themselves.

Mother needs love too and lets the family know
by slamming the bedroom door and retreating
to the other side. When the house is finally
still, the dog wanders from room to room
wagging her tail, bone in mouth,
looking for someone who will dare take it away.

REVENGE

after the painting, *Self-Portrait,*
by Judith Leyster, 1632-33

If she could she would tell us
the small portrait in her painting
used to be of her when she was a girl
but she thought twice about it—
the public would think her too indulgent
and what of Rembrandt and his cronies?
Lastman came on to her last week saying
there are better positions for women
than standing in front of an easel.
She clears the small portrait
and decides to paint the fiddler—
the silly imp all the men paint
to show off their penises—
but her brush will be a dagger
as she clutches the palette
and refuses to let go.

SCHADENFREUDE

When I get my hair cut Eddie lathers me
with 30 minutes of local disasters:
a man falls down the elevator shaft of the building
we're in and plunges to his death,
a boy in Tracy chained down for a year
in his foster parents' garage,
a San Francisco woman mauled by a pit bull.
When I leave I promise myself
I'll find another barber but still I return
to my live edition of the *Enquirer*:
when the hair dryer stops I'm thankful
I've only been imagining an oncoming train.

LOOKING GLASS

A man is weeping in the back of the #10 MUNI.
During staff meetings, the executives text: sound of
   rodents scurrying.

A pregnant soldier is killed by a psychiatrist in Ft. Hood.
The Berlin Wall: 20 years later, a boy jumps across the
   imaginary divide.

In an e-mail, a man attempts to tell his boss the truth.
Bytes stream through buildings—nothing but 0's and 1's.

A homeless woman is in a tirade on the corner of Folsom
   and Fifth.
On a church billboard: *We don't change the message. The
message changes us.*

A man sees his reflection in a lingerie store window and stops.
In the ballet, a woman in a wheelchair reaches out, and
   another dancer takes her hand.

THE WEAPON

A man was apprehended in a coffee shop after a hold-up. It turned out his gun was a banana and he ate it in front of the police.
—NPR, May 2009

Perhaps he intended to eat the banana all along
but he was just scammed and something cracked
when he was standing by the register,
the cash easy prey—the same moment each of us has
when the impossible suddenly becomes possible:
the time I confronted the shopkeeper in Kabul
because the shirt I bought the day before shrank into a rag.
He pretended he didn't know me and when I blurted
I'll buy a new one, I became an old friend.
He pulled out a stack, I bolted with the one on top
and he gave chase with a pole shouting *Allah ak-bar*.
A flash of vengeance because the booty is there—
and for a moment a banana will make things right.

THE WAY

The dog with cancer lies on the couch as the family
has dinner. The girls can't stop talking about
their plans for the weekend—parties, a concert with
The Lovemakers—the kids they like and dislike.
Father insists they say something positive
about the kids they don't like, how the traits
we don't care for in others reflect back
on ourselves. Someone knocks on the door
but the dog does not bark.

• • •

A woman boards MUNI and yells at the driver
when he asks for proof of her handicap.
I don't need to do shit for you white people anymore.
Have one son and he's serving your fucking Navy
in Iraq. Fucking shit. You think you rule the world.
Can't you see I'm limping. Hit by a car when I cross
Mission. White car. Trash has no insurance.
Everyone on the bus is quiet. A man flips
the page of his *Chronicle* and everyone turns.

• • •

In the Temple of the Eight Immortals a man
walks through halls filled with patchouli incense,
stops in front of a bronze Buddha-like god,
red lips a reluctant smile. Nearby a priest chants
from the *Tao Te Ching*, each breath a string
of musical notes. The man leaves and comes back
with a strip of paper: Chinese characters that resemble
a couple embracing, two people walking, a dancer.
The man hands the strip to the priest and begins to weep.

DOG WITH THREE LEGS

We walk her up the steps during an otherwise splendid
urban dusk, the sky clear but occluded by human light—

the limb now just a wound held together by staples,
the incision an imperfect semicircle but

perfect in its intention: the quick removal
of the leg diseased with cancer. The dog seems

oblivious, stopping every so often to lick the wound,
her world suddenly a tripod,

her sense of balance redefined but unquestioned.
When she stops she looks up at us for

encouragement, her tail wagging but not
in the usual happy way—it's curled behind her

like a comma, a pause before she lifts her front leg
and places it onto the next ascending step.

OPENING

A book of photographs by blind teenagers.
The aperture opens: a split second of light.

An *a capella* group sings a Serb war song about unrequited love.
The Belgrade zoo is bombed: polar bears wander to the Sava River.

A dream where I divorce my mother.
When my sister and I become teens, our small room is halved:
    two dollhouses.

The phone keeps ringing in the middle of the night.
For the dying, time is endless.

At the cemetery my dog barks at the stone angels.
On Rilke's tombstone: *To be nobody's sleep under so many eyelids.*

NOTES

"Hired Help"
gribenes: chicken or goose skin cracklings with fried onions;
schmaltz: rendered chicken or goose fat

"Green Balloons"
Wir können jetzt glücklich sein: We can be happy now.

"Mother Wants to Know"
Ich bin froh das ich hier bin: I'm happy that I'm here.

"Statement Recording the Property of Jews"
Kalbsbraten: veal roast; *Spätzle:* small noodles or dumplings

"Artifact"
Tefillin: a set of small cubic leather boxes painted black, containing scrolls of parchment inscribed with verses from the *Torah*. They have leather straps dyed black on one side, and are worn by observant Jews during weekday morning prayers.

"Hubert, 1990"
Wir haben von nichts gewusst: We didn't know about anything.

"Midrash"
Heimat : homeland

"Vigil: Finishing the Barn"
La Migra: immigration police
¡No he visto a mi bebé en cuatro meses!: I haven't seen my baby in four months!
Cada niño necesita a su papa: Every boy needs his dad.

"Dog at the Dining Table"
Bois de Boulogne: a park located along the western edge of the
16th arrondissement of Paris

"Voyage"
Ile St. Louis: one of the two natural islands in the Seine River,
in Paris

"The Flat-Footed American"
hutong: a traditional alley or courtyard, most commonly found
in Beijing

"Unfinished"
Ljubljanica: a river in Slovenia. The capital, Ljubljana, is situated
on the river.

"Opatiya"
Lungomare: a beachside promenade in Opatiya, Croatia

"Woman Playing the Theorbo"
theorbo: a plucked string instrument developed during the late
16th century
hutspot: a Dutch dish of mashed potatoes, carrots, and onions

"Schadenfreude"
Schadenfreude: pleasure derived from the misfortunes of others

"The Weapon"
Allah ak-bar: God is great

About the Photographer

Leon Borenzstein is an internationally renowned photographer whose work has appeared in *Life, Harper's, The New York Times Magazine,* and *Vogue International.* He has had one-person exhibitions at Yerba Buena Center for the Arts, San Francisco; the Cleveland Art Museum; Centre Nationale de la Photographie, Paris; Fraenkel Gallery, San Francisco; and others. A project with the Oakland Creative Growth Center produced the book *One is Adam, One is Superman* in 2004. His photographs can be found in the collections of major museums such as the Art Institute of Chicago; Biblioteque Nationale, Paris; Museum of Fine Arts, Houston; and the San Francisco Museum of Modern Art. He received a 2003 California Council for the Humanities grant and a 1987 Guggenheim Memorial Fellowship. He teaches at the San Francisco Art Institute and lives in Oakland, California.

About the Author

Stewart Florsheim was born in New York City, the son of refugees from Hitler's Germany. He has received several awards for his poetry and was recently nominated for a Pushcart Prize. He has been widely published in magazines and anthologies. Stewart was the editor of *Ghosts of the Holocaust*, an anthology of poetry by children of Holocaust survivors (Wayne State University Press, 1989). He wrote the poetry chapbook, *The Girl Eating Oysters* (2River, 2004). In 2005, Stewart won the Blue Light Book Award for *The Short Fall From Grace* (Blue Light Press, 2006). He has been awarded residencies from Artcroft and the Kimmel Harding Nelson Center for the Arts. Stewart also writes non-fiction. Stewart's day job is in the technical writing field. He is also co-chair of the Board of Directors of Compassion & Choices of Northern California, an organization that helps the terminally ill make end-of-life decisions. Stewart lives in the Bay Area with his wife, two daughters, and their dog, Roxie.

ALSO BY STEWART FLORSHEIM

Ghosts of the Holocaust (editor) (1989)
The Girl Eating Oysters (2004)
The Short Fall from Grace (2006)

Printed in the United States of America

www.ingramcontent.com/pod-product-compliance
Lightning Source LLC
Chambersburg PA
CBHW032020090426
42741CB00006B/675